Generational Information

A Brief Guide for
Teaching Millennial Learners

D0107561

J. Bradley Garner

TRIANGLE PUBLISHING

A Brief Guide for Teaching Millennial Learners
J. Bradley Garner

Direct correspondence and permission requests to one of the following:

E-mail:	info@trianglepublishing.com
Web site:	www.trianglepublishing.com
Mail:	Triangle Publishing
	1900 W. 50th Street
	Marion, Indiana 46953
	USA

J. Bradley Garner
A Brief Guide for Teaching Millennial Learners

Graphic design: Lyn Rayn

ISBN: 978-1-931283-26-7

Printed in the United States of America

Contents

Time for a Change

❦

B efore you begin reading this text, take a few minutes to participate in a virtual field trip. Imagine that you have just entered the hallway of an academic building on a college campus of your choosing anywhere in the world. Now picture yourself walking down that hallway during a time of the day when classes are in session. Stop and listen. What do you hear? There is a high probability that the most prevalent sound is a faculty member's voice delivering a lecture or monologue. Although there may be brief interludes of conversation and dialogue around the topic at hand, the professor's voice is almost universally the foremost sound emanating from our classrooms.

Let's now continue with the second part of this virtual field trip. As you walk further down the hall, take a moment to look into a classroom and observe the behavior, posture, and attentiveness of the students. What do you see in their eyes? What does their body language tell you? Do their facial expressions give you any indication of their level of involvement and engagement in the learning process? Be aware that the faces you are seeing in these classrooms are a new generation of learners often referred to as "millennials." Quite often, their looks of passivity and resignation reflect a variety of feelings including fatigue, boredom, disinterest, and/or capitulation to their required physical presence (but conceivably optional mental engagement).

I have conducted this virtual experiment with groups of college faculty on numerous occasions literally around the world. In every trial their responses are remarkably consistent with those described above. Spence (2001) described a retrospective version of the virtual experiment that you have just completed:

> For just a moment, assume that time travel is possible. Plop a medieval peasant in a modern dairy farm and he would recognize nothing but the cows. A physician of the 13th century would run screaming from a modern operating room. Galileo could only gape and mutter touring NASA's Johnson Space Center. Columbus would quake with terror in a nuclear sub. But a 15th century teacher from the University of Paris would feel right at home in a Berkeley classroom. (p. 13)

These scenarios invoke thoughts about one of the controversies in higher education and the best ways to facilitate student learning in a 21st century college classroom (Barr & Tagg, 1995; Braskamp, Trautvetter, & Ward, 2006; Tagg, 2003).   Of course there are many opinions on the best response to this dilemma. After all, as Spence has observed, our current way of doing business has served us well for at least the past 600 years (and probably longer). The time has come for a change. Hutchings and Shulman (1999) have echoed the relative permanence that exists within the academy:

> Since the 1990s, American colleges and universities have initiated numerous efforts to improve teaching and learning on their campuses. These efforts have resulted in an expanded repertoire of teaching practices, including greater student involvement through collaborative and cooperative learning; technology-based teaching; service-learning; role-playing to promote active classrooms; learning communities to bring faculty and students closer together; and teaching centers to improve practice. . . . And yet, for all the pedagogical innovations — even the advent of the Web — there has been precious little deeper reform. Individual professors may teach somewhat differently than they did two decades ago and discussions about how to assess learning are more common than in the past, but there is little evidence that the changes

add up to systematic reconsideration of how and why students learn or how institutions, rather than simply individual professors, can revise their approaches to teaching. (p. 13)

This is a grim analysis for the prospect of change in the academy. However, on a more personal level, consider one of the worst-case scenarios of teaching at the college level. There you are, standing in front of a classroom looking into the eyes of your students. As you glance at your notes, and then at your watch, you realize that another twenty minutes remain in the class period. Simultaneously, you survey the classroom. There you see what you most dread: blank stares, drooping eyes, heads that appear too heavy to support their own weight, uncontrollable doodling, window/door gazing, and compulsive clock watching. It is a helpless feeling. You continue to talk, knowing that your words and wonderfully clever thoughts are drifting off into the atmosphere, never to connect with the hearts and minds of your students. What you are observing and experiencing are the classic symptoms of *Lecture Induced Mind Paralysis*.

The primary purpose of this text is to provide college faculty members with a collection of strategies and techniques that are effective antidotes against the ravages of Lecture Induced Mind Paralysis. Am I suggesting the heretical view that lectures have absolutely no place in the college classroom? Absolutely not! As will be illustrated, however, I am fervently advocating for the advancement of a pedagogy that includes the lecture as *one* among *many* tools, techniques and approaches that maybe used by college faculty which provide students with multiple avenues for learning.

Are you convinced? Will you join the growing army of faculty who are dedicated to quelling the spread of Lecture Induced Mind Paralysis? In either case, my suggestion is that you take a bold step and continue reading. Take one or two of the many techniques that described in this book and try them in your own classroom. My belief is that you will experience a new and more energetic response from your students.

How This Text is Organized

Teaching is hard work. It requires faculty members to draw upon their own abilities to process, evaluate, and synthesize information from a variety of sources. To provide a backdrop for our exploration of the teaching process, and to give us a context for our exploration, we will use the analogy of preparing for and giving a performance. This analogy is not intended to put emphasis on the "edutainment" value of teaching (Marinelli & Pausch, 2004), but rather to emphasize that any excellent performance (e.g., play, movie, concert) is dependent upon a number of important variables including the set, script, technical components, and a review of the final work.

Setting the Stage

Much of what we see on a stage or a movie screen is the result of countless hours of meticulous planning, preparation, and rehearsal. Good teaching also requires that faculty members think through and plan the intricate details of the learning time with their students. Many (but not all) of the pitfalls and challenges of teaching are rather predictable. Time spent in the preparation of a syllabus and planning the sequence of instruction is a worthy investment. In this section of the text, we will focus on preemptive strategies that can save you pain, heartache, and frustration as the semester begins.

Optimizing Classroom Teaching Performance

Although good teaching clearly goes beyond the boundaries of the classroom, as we develop relationships with our students and build into their lives through mentoring and advising, it is within the classroom that we take on a major role in helping our students acquire the knowledge, skills, and dispositions of the discipline. The amount of time allotted to a semester of instruction is finite. It is the obligation of faculty members to maximize and effectively use the allotted time to best advantage. The primary goal of the following collection of strategies is to energize the classroom and enhance the learning process through student engagement.

Learning from your Reviews

The mark of a great teacher is the ability to process and analyze what is happening in the teaching moment, but also reflect on what worked and what didn't. There will be days when you leave the classroom and say to yourself "This was a disaster. I will never do that again!" However, on other days, you will be jumping for joy as you reflect on the amazing level of insight development, interaction, and engagement that you observed in the eyes and words of your students. Both types of days will plague you for the remainder of your teaching career. Get used to it... but also learn from these experiences as they will make you a more effective teacher. We will focus on a variety of approaches that can be taken to assess the learning and skill acquisition of your students. The quality and quantity of student learning that occurs in your classroom is a meaningful way of assessing the quality of your teaching.

How to Use this Text

A goal that I have in writing this text is that if I meet you somewhere, and you have a copy of this book, that it will be tattered, torn, and well used. That is not an expression of my vanity (although it does clearly exist), but rather a hope that this will be a book that you use in your work as a college faculty member.

This is not a book that you will or should read from cover to cover (unless you have a persistent case of insomnia). Rather, think of it as a toolbox that contains a variety of examples, techniques, and strategies that you can choose and skillfully apply in your classroom, based upon the circumstances and the needs of your students. My most sincere hope is that you will find ways to add to the list of strategies contained in this book from the depth of your greatest teaching resource . . . your own experience and creativity.

In addition to the following text you can also access my regular web tools at http://www.indwes.edu/TheToolBox.

Brad Garner
Associate Dean for Teaching and Learning
Indiana Wesleyan University, brad.garner@indwes.edu

CHAPTER ONE

Welcome the Millennial Learners

Meet the Millennials, born in or after 1982 — the "Babies on Board" of the early Reagan years, the "Have You Hugged Your Child Today?" sixth graders of the early Clinton years, the teens of Columbine . . . now invading the nation's campuses.

As a group, Millennials are unlike any other youth generation in living memory. They are more numerous, more affluent, better educated, and more ethnically diverse. More important, they are beginning to manifest a wide array of positive social habits that older Americans no longer associate with youth, including a new focus on teamwork, achievement, modesty, and good conduct. Only a few years from now, this can-do youth revolution will overwhelm cynics and pessimists. Over the next decade, the Millennial Generation will entirely recast the image of youth from downbeat and alienated to upbeat and engaged—with potentially seismic consequences. (Howe & Strauss, 2000, p. 4)

There is an ever-increasing buzz about the millennial generation and their potential impact on the world as we know it. For example, a review of recent publications indicates a high level of interest in the possible ways that this "new" generation will affect current practices in retail sales (Reda, 2006), parenting practices (Jayson, 2006), leadership (Downing, 2006), broadcasting (Romano, 2006), fashion (Seckler, 2006), advertising (Bosman, 2006), finances (Brandenburg, 2005), and corporate management (Nelson, 2005). Additionally, as you might expect, the millennials are also poised to make a dramatic impact on higher education (Howe & Strauss, 2003). It would serve faculty members well to take notice of this new group of students and begin to think seriously about instructional practices that would be most responsive to their learning needs (Braskamp, Trautvetter, & Ward, 2006; Garner, 2007; Garner & Pattengale, 2007; Millard, 2007; Twenge, 2006).

To illustrate the tension that can exist between millennial learners and instructional practices in higher education, consider the role of technology as a life influence. Let's begin this exploration by thinking back to the early 1980s. What do you remember about the level of technology that you used on a regular basis? Cell phones were not yet on the scene, laserdiscs were the big news in video, and the Sony Walkman led the way in audio. Personal computers were just beginning to become part of the landscape. In the early 80s, Apple introduced the Macintosh computer, Radio Shack proudly announced the arrival of the TRS-80, and the Commodore 64 was on the scene. This was also roughly the year that marked the beginning of what we now call the millennial generation. Think for a moment about the technological developments that have been introduced over that twenty-five year period — developments that have become an integral part of our vocabulary, our lives, and our culture:

- Widespread, almost universal, increases in the availability and use of computers
- A cell phone for every ear in America
- Pagers, Personal Digital Assistants (PDAs), CDs, DVDs, MP3s
- iPods, Podcasts, and Smartphones
- Video games and an amazing variety of video game devices
- Internet sites, email, instant messaging, blogs, and chat rooms

- PowerPoint presentations and LCD projectors
- New language terms including net surfing, information superhighway, web site, chat room, cyber, browser, online, homepage, HTML, and @

It is no surprise that millennial students are often categorized as "digital natives", while the rest of us, who can actually remember the unveiling of the TRS-80 are cast into the role of "digital immigrants" (Prensky, 2001).

Millennials, raised their entire lives in a culture that celebrates and covets the most recent, quickest, flashiest, smallest, and most convenient form of technology of the moment, have become accustomed to integrating that technology into every aspect of their lives. For them technology is simply a fact of life:

> A new generation of students has arrived. . . . They carry an arsenal of electronic devices — the more portable the better. Raised amid a barrage of information, they are able to juggle a conversation on Instant Messenger, a Web-surfing session, and an iTunes playlist while reading Twelfth Night for homework. Whether or not they are absorbing the fine points of the play is a matter of debate. (Scott, 2005, A34)

The unique qualities of millennials go beyond their affinity for an electronic connection (Howe & Strauss, 2006; Twenge, 2006). Consider for a moment the histories and life narratives of the learners that are sitting in your classroom. They come to college with a unique collection of experiences more diverse than any previous generation of college students. Howe and Strauss (2000), in their exhaustive review of this new generation, propose a range of descriptors to capture the essence and personality of millennials:

- They're optimists . . .
- They're cooperative team players . . .
- They accept authority . . .
- They're rule followers . . .
- They're the most watched over generation in memory . . .

- They're smarter than most people think . . .
- Today's kids believe in the future and see themselves as its cutting edge. (pp. 7-10)

These, of course, are generalizations about a large group of individuals. This list provides, however, some insight into the nature of our students. The challenge for college faculty becomes one of understanding this new breed of learners and creating a range of teaching techniques that is responsive to their needs and styles. The most commonly cited list of millennial attributes comes from the work of Howe and Strauss (2000). According to these seminal generational gurus, millennials are:

- **Special** (i.e., as a focal point of societal and parental focus)
- **Sheltered** (i.e, under the auspices of "helicopter parents")
- **Confident** (i.e., "We can make a difference")
- **Team-Oriented** (i.e., the good of the group is critically important)
- **Conventional** (i.e., attracted to traditions)
- **Pressured** (i.e., working hard to achieve)
- **Achieving** (i.e., expected and expecting to do great things).

As you proceed through the remaining chapters of this text, you will review a variety of instructional strategies that have been intentionally field tested and selected for millennial learners. The rationale for this selection process is based upon several key criteria that you may wish to consider as you think about your own teaching: 1) Active engagement, 2) Hands-on experiences, and 3) Varied formats for connecting with the learning process.

Active Engagement

Millennials, as a group, tend to be attracted to learning opportunities that involve interaction, discussion, information processing, and dialogue about real-life issues and concerns of their world. Although there will always be a need to create strategies for students to acquire the core knowledge base of your academic discipline (i.e., reading, listening to lectures), faculty members should be mindful of the need to intentionally incorporate problem solving, brainstorming, and discussion into the mix of a classroom session.

Hands-On Experiences

The opportunity to be out in the world, try out new skills, talk with practitioners of the discipline, and get their hands dirty in community settings is a critically important part of the learning process. The dynamics of this opportunity are clear:

- It is one thing to read about a key principle in political science, it is quite another to visit the state capital and talk with legislators.
- It is one thing to learn about the criminal justice system, it is quite another to make a visit to a prison and talk with correction officers.
- It is one thing to listen to a lecture about the impact of homelessness, it is quite another to serve meals at a soup kitchen.

Consider finding ways to provide your students with opportunities to actively apply what you are teaching in a variety of contexts.

Varied Formats for Connecting with the Learning Process

Millennials appreciate the opportunity to make choices about the ways in which they learn. That does not imply that faculty should hand over course content and requirements to the class or that expectations for learning should be lowered. Rather, by providing students with a variety of ways to meet course requirements (e.g., projects, interviews, examinations, service learning, movie reviews, extra reading assignments of fictional literature related to course content), faculty are empowering students to make choices based upon their own self-awareness about learning styles and interests. To put this in perspective:

- You can't teach your students everything that you know about your discipline.

- You are the person in the best position to identify the direction, focus and quantity of content that will be covered. Take seriously your power and ability to determine the most cogent and significant knowledge, skills, and dispositions that you will emphasize over the course of the semester.

Although you are the master of content choices, consider empowering students in regard to how they acquire, process, and master that content.

A Top Ten List for Working with Millennials

Although we will further develop this theme while considering a variety of classroom teaching and learning techniques, I am taking this opportunity to realize one of my own dreams: to create a top ten list. Fans of David Letterman are familiar with this staple of his television show that features ten observations about a wide variety of topics. With that introduction, consider my "Top Ten List for Working with Millennials":

#10   **Invest your time in getting to know the narratives that are the life stories of your students** — Find ways to connect with your students outside of class. Begin to learn their individual stories and share yours. This simple commitment turns the classroom into a group of people that you know (and who know you) rather than a sea of faces.

#9   **Think outside the box of traditional classroom routines and structures** — Think of each class session as an experiment and adventure in learning. Try new things, take a chance, do something new this week. What is the worst thing that could happen?

#8   **Intentionally connect content with practice** — Always ask yourself the "So what?" and "Now what?" questions. These questions help us evaluate the content of what we are teaching (i.e., "Is all of this really that important?") and how we are connecting the content to real world scenarios (i.e., "Here's how this information is playing itself out in the world-at-large").

#7 **Use technology wisely and judiciously** — As has been noted, millennials are technologically savvy. We all need to take the time and effort to enhance our own abilities to effectively use technology in the classroom. Remember, however, technology is not an end in itself. It is a tool that can enhance learning, not a substitution for good planning and good classroom conversation.

#6 **Create narratives** — Millennials love stories. Great stories are all around us. Use stories (e.g., historical accounts, letters, movies, plays, fictional literature) as a way of breathing life into your teaching. Narratives provide a context for our teaching. Narratives also provide a touch point for students to make connections between the course content and their own unique narratives.

#5 **Incorporate varied strategies for group work** — Millennials generally love to work in groups. This is a fact that can pay great dividends in the classroom because working in groups is one of the most effective ways to facilitate the processing and application of newly acquired knowledge, skills, and dispositions. As a means of holding yourself accountable in this area, set a limit on the number of PowerPoint slides that you use during each class session or the maximum number of minutes that you will engage in a monologue. Given this newly available time, how will you spend it wisely? What kinds of group discussion topics might amplify and magnify the class topic for the day?

#4 **Look at your students with high expectations in mind** — Is the glass half-full or half-empty? It is easy to get caught up in the dialogue that leads to the conclusion that students don't care, their skills are declining, they don't come to college to learn, etc. Resist the temptation to be part of these discussions. As a faculty member, you have the power and the ability to influence their learning and their lives. Use this power by setting high expectations and being a coach and facilitator who helps each student move toward those lofty goals. That is the essence of the teaching and learning paradigm.

#3   Talk less — You do know a whole bunch of stuff about your discipline. That is good news. There is no obligation, however, to say it all over the course of a semester. Try thinking of your role as one of helping students find the answers to the most important questions in your field. This requires the composition of excellent questions that lead students to think, inquire, and analyze. Another part of this formula is to wait for the answers to the questions that you ask. Resist the temptation to jump in and answer your own questions and take students off the hook as they sit in a silent classroom (waiting for someone to answer). As a short-term goal, try to reduce the amount of direct talking and lecture that you do by 20%. You will be amazed at how much your students have to say and the number of questions that they have to ask. Their speaking and asking can also lead to learning.

#2   Only make rules that you are willing to enforce — Millennials generally have a keen sense of fairness. They generally respect authority and the rules. Your job becomes one of deciding which rules are really important and worthy of diligent enforcement and which rules are just rules for the sake of having a rule.

(And now imagine a drum roll . . .)

#1   Show you care, share your passion — Over the past several years, I have had the pleasure of taking a group of students from our campus to visit a local residential facility for adolescents with emotional and behavioral challenges. The students spend time tutoring and mentoring the residents at this facility As we drive in the van from our campus to the residential facility, the students talk about a variety of topics but invariably spend some of that time talking about the faculty they are working with that semester. As they are having those conversations, I become invisible. They talk quite openly about what they like and what they don't like about various faculty members. Two clear characteristics consistently emerge as they describe the faculty members that they admire the most and are most interested in learning from: They care for their students and they have a passion for their subject matter. Be that teacher!

CHAPTER TWO

Setting the Stage

Once a semester begins, time seems to fly. It is a sprint from the beginning to the end. Quite often, we find ourselves responding to the circumstances of the moment. In spite of the rush and pace of the academic year, it is critically important for faculty members to allot the time necessary to effectively plan the academic experiences they envision for their students. This planning process sets the stage for you and for your students. As you prepare a syllabus that includes many important pieces of information for the semester ahead (e.g., your expectations for student participation, the schedule of topics that will be addressed, due dates for assignments, attendance policies) you are laying the groundwork for a well-designed learning experience. This preliminary work will be appreciated by your students and will ultimately add value and coherence to the overall learning experience.

In this chapter, we will review some of the basic aspects of course design that you can consider and address prior to the beginning of the semester:

- Building a syllabus
- Encouraging students to read their textbooks
- Enforcing attendance policies
- Setting expectations for classroom civility

Building a Syllabus

A staple of higher education is the creation of course syllabi. As routine as this process may sound, or even become, the development of thorough, complete, and well-conceived course syllabi can provide the groundwork for a successful semester of 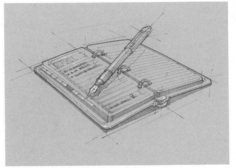 learning. According to Slattery and Carlson (2005), citing the work of Littlefield (1999), there are seven major functions of the course syllabus. A high quality syllabus . . .

- **Sets the tone for the course** — A well developed course syllabus sends the important message that the faculty member has given serious thought to course organization and delivery. A syllabus that is attractive, and well organized, and that captures the interest of students from the first day of class will pay benefits throughout the semester.
- **Motivates students to set high goals for themselves** — If students sense your excitement, passion, and commitment to the content of the course, they are more likely to be willing to stretch themselves to achieve and produce. Consider your syllabus as an invitation to your students — an invitation to give their best efforts and to get your best efforts. Expect great things from your students and give them great teaching in exchange.
- **Serves as a planning tool** — A high quality syllabus sets forth the teacher's game plan for the semester. As you go through the process of developing your course syllabus, you are additionally afforded the opportunity to plan your instructional strategies for the semester.

Syllabus Preparation Checklist

❑ **General Information:** This introductory section of the syllabus provides such basic information as the course title, section number(s), classroom location, dates and times of class meetings, and faculty contact information (e.g., telephone numbers, email addresses), required texts and course materials and your office hours.

❑ **Course Rationale:** This is your opportunity to share the reasons why this course is a critically important and how the content connects with the life and learning experiences of your students.

❑ **Your Passion and Purpose in Teaching This Course:** Share your personal and professional passion for this course and the things that will be taught and learned. Share your heart and your faith with your students.

❑ **Course Objectives:** Articulate the knowledge, skills, and dispositions that you believe are important for your students to master over the course of this semester.

❑ **Topical Schedule:** How do you plan to approach the breadth and depth of the topics that comprise this area of study? In this section of the syllabus, provide your students a dated schedule of the topics that you will be covering on this semester long adventure.

❑ **Course Reading:** Students are not genetically and naturally inclined to read required course materials. Through your prompting and systematic planning, however, they can be encouraged to see the value of reading along as they are learning.

❑ **Course Assignments:** Students need to know in detail what it is that you will expect them to produce this semester, the parameters of those assignments, and when they are due to be completed. Although some may choose to procrastinate, for others it gives an important target date for task completion.

❑ **Assessment Scheme:** "Will this be on the test?" is a common refrain of the college classroom. Prepare in advance for the assessment strategies that you will use (e.g., quizzes and examinations, research papers, group projects, presentations, on-line activities). Provide your students with information on these tasks and their relative levels of importance (e.g., point values).

❑ **Course/University Policies:** What are the policies and procedures that your students need to understand as they enter this course? Examples include attendance procedures, reasonable and acceptable absences, and cheating/academic dishonesty. Spell these out in your syllabus or give reference points so that students can remain well informed.

❑ **Motivational Thoughts:** As an added touch, consider the use of graphics, and text boxes with quotes that connect with your course and your teaching.

❑ **Additional Resources and Assistance:** Provide students with resources or information on how to get additional assistance they may need, appropriate internet links, and campus resources that will assist in their learning.

- **Provides a structure for student work** — You are competing for the time, interest, and energies of your students. A well-conceived syllabus communicates your expectation that students will invest themselves in meeting the learning requirements of your course. This provision also encourages students to look ahead and plan effective ways to complete assigned tasks.
- **Helps faculty plan and meet course requirements and expectations** — Planning time spent in advance of the semester (e.g., order of approaching topics, timing of assignments, planning in regard to instructional activities) will pay dividends in the quality of your teaching. You have a sense of where you are headed and can lead your students — learning in that clear direction.
- **Provides a contractual arrangement between faculty and students** — Any disagreements that may arise concerning grading practices, due dates, and attendance policies can be referred back to the stated course policies and procedures.
- **Becomes a portfolio artifact for promotion** — As time passes and you prepare for promotion and the preparation of a portfolio, course syllabi serve as a means for documenting the quality of your teaching and the ways in which you addressed the learning needs of your students.

As you plan for the semester ahead, consider using this syllabus planner as a template for the types of information that you include.

A Unique Approach: The A La Carte Syllabus

Imagine that you are extremely hungry and have just been given the opportunity to partake of a meal at one of your favorite restaurants. The food at this eatery is extraordinary! You have decided to throw caution to the wind and ignore the everyday concerns about calories, fat content, and carbohydrates. As the waiter approaches, you struggle with what to order because there are several items on the menu that you really enjoy. You hesitate, and then describe your dilemma to the waiter. Much to your surprise, he invites you to simply pick and choose from a variety of meal options based upon your own personal preferences. You choose a meal that meets your own needs and preferences. Let the meal begin, even though you will be sorry tomorrow! Consider this illustration in relation to course design and student learning. As teachers, we all strive to provide instructional opportunities that will maximize the degree to which our students gain new information, understanding, skills, and concepts. Quite often, however, course syllabi reveal a "one size fits all" mentality. Although we know that each of our students learn differently and bring varied levels of competence and skill to the classroom, everyone is required to complete identical assignments and tasks over the course of a semester. This observation is particularly applicable to millennials who have a strong preference for learning activities that include options for choice and for setting their own paths to learning.

There is an alternative — teaching a la carte! In this approach to course design (Thompson and Grabau, 2004):

- Individual differences are acknowledged
- The demonstration of learning can occur in a variety of ways
- Students are provided with an opportunity to select their own learning activities from a menu of choices

The implementation of teaching a la carte requires three easy steps:

Step One
Identify those basic learning activities and course requirements that you believe all students should complete. Examples might include reading the assigned text, class attendance, engagement in classroom discussions, or participation in tests, quizzes, and examinations.

Sample Menu

The following is a list of potential items that could be included in a learning menu (along with some ideas regarding point values based upon a 1000 point scale). The reader will need to judge the relevance of these activities to their own discipline or the degree to which they should be modified.

Interviews of Professionals in the Field (200 points)

Interview a minimum of three professionals currently employed in the human services field (e.g., teacher, social worker, psychologist, probation officer). Prepare a summary of your interviews, synthesizing the data obtained and generating relevant conclusions and observations.

Research Paper (200 points)

Write a research paper on one of the following topics (or one that is pre-approved by the instructor) Your research paper should be five or more pages in length (word processed, 12 pt. font, double spaced, 1 inch margin on top bottom and sides). Include a reference page citing a minimum of six references from the professional literature (with emphasis on articles appearing in professional journals). A rubric will be provided to specify guidelines and grading expectations.

Video Reviews (200 points possible)

Watch 8 videos/DVDs that relate to the topic/content of this course. Provide a written review of each video/DVD using the approved format.

Read One of the Following Books (200 points possible)

Write a three page essay containing the following components: 1) Basic thesis of the book, 2) A section of the book that had the greatest impact on you as a person, 3) Spiritual applications and connections to your faith in God and 4) Implications of this book for you as a human service professional.

Shadow a Professional in the Field (200 points possible)

Shadow a professional in the area or field of human services that you are considering as a focus for your vocation/calling. Journalize your experiences and those insights.

Develop a resource notebook (150 points possible)

Develop a resource notebook of materials that will be useful to you. The resource notebook should be a minimum of 100 pages of content selected from a variety of sources. Organize these resources with topical dividers.

Share A Motivational Comment with the Class (150 points)

As a means of integrating your personal narrative with your new knowledge and information, prepare a motivational comment for presentation to the class. The presentation should be 5-7 minutes in length and may take the form of a story, illustration, interpretive reading, song, dramatic presentation, etc. Make a connection between course content education and your personal story. A rubric will be provided. This assignment can be completed individually or in a group of two or three.

Create a PowerPoint Presentation (150 points)

Take some aspect of course content and develop a PowerPoint presentation that illustrates an important principle or concept. The presentation can only include a maximum of 10 pictures and 25 words. Be creative.

Provide Volunteer Experiences (150 points)

Provide 15 hours of volunteer services related to course content. Maintain a journal describing the nature of your volunteer services and the things that you are experiencing and learning.

Design Your Own Project (To be determined)

Submit a written description that includes the following components: 1) Summary of project activities, 2) Estimated time expenditure, and 3) Method/product for sharing results.

Step Two

Create a "menu" of additional learning activities that students can choose from as a way of demonstrating their learning and their ability to apply the information that they are gaining through their reading and participation in class. A sample menu is included on the previous page.

Step Three

Assign point values to the various required and optional experiences that will comprise your assessment system. For example, based upon a 1000 point system, students would be presented with the following alternatives:

- Readings in textbook   100 points (required)
- Class attendance   100 points (required)
- Quizzes   100 points (required)
- Mid-Term Examination   100 points (required)
- Final Examination   100 points (required)
- Choices from the "menu"   500 points (of the students' choosing)

Under this proposed arrangement, students can select several activities that total 1000 points (or more if they so choose). At the end of the semester, the total number of points that students accrue (from required and selected items) will determine their final grade in the course.

What about Textbooks?

One of the essential components of a college education is (or should be) the textbook. Traditionally, it is thought, students sign up for their courses and then make that dreaded trek to the bookstore where they pay large sums of money to purchase their textbooks. The other part of that story is the assumption (dare we

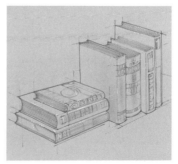

say "fantasy") of faculty members that students will actually read and digest the content of those purchased textbooks in some meaningful and lasting way. To be sure, textbooks are often considered part of the culture of a college campus. Large, heavy textbooks are portrayed as the calling card of a scholarly life. There is reason, however, to take a critical view of reality about the assumptions guiding the use and selection of textbooks and their overall role in the learning process.

Assumption #1: Textbook production is a moneymaking industry.
First and foremost, the people who publish and sell textbooks are in the business of generating profit. Their business is highly dependent upon attracting the attention of faculty members for the purpose of textbook adoption. This is accomplished by clever marketing and the immediate availability of examination copies, website resources, and prefabricated test question banks.   This observation does not demean the textbook publishing industry. It does, however, reinforce the idea of "Let the Buyer Beware." Be a wise and careful consumer and textbook adopter.

Assumption #2: Textbooks are a vital and integral part of the learning process.
There is good reason to believe that this assumption is accurate. Quite often, courses are designed and offered in deference to the content and organizational structures found in the textbooks chosen by faculty. The sequence of events that typically transpires is:

- Faculty members select textbooks which provide the best coverage of the topics included in the course
- Lectures and tests are designed in accordance with the sequence of chapters found in the chosen textbooks
- The course schedule is created based upon the sequence of chapters as they appear in the textbooks

The logical next question becomes whether these decisions about textbook selection influence student learning in the ways that we might envision and hope to realize.

Assumption #3: Students actually read their textbooks.

The research available on the textbook reading habits of college students is remarkably scarce. What is available, however, is rather disturbing. A study by Connor-Greene (2000) revealed that 72% of surveyed students never read their assignments by the due date. In another study, Sikorski, et al (2002) found that as many as 30% of the students surveyed indicated that they did not purchase any texts for at least one of their scheduled courses. Clump, Bauer, and Bradley (2004) report that many college students spend less than 3 hours per week reading assigned textbook materials.

Assumption #4: The ultimate question is "Will this be on the test?"

Although many students are committed to learning, there is also a sizeable group of students who are interested in doing only what is necessary to "pass" certain courses. One question to consider, however, is the source of the questions that are "on the test." Do they come from class lectures, the text or both? One way of encouraging students to read their textbooks is to clearly send the message that information contained in their textbooks in critically important . . . important enough to warrant reading the assigned texts.

How Can We Get Students to Read Their Textbooks?

Here are some strategies designed to increase the likelihood that your students will take advantage of the reading materials that are included in your courses:

Assign Course-Related Point Values to Assigned Readings

Surprisingly, and quite often, the expectation that students are actually required to read the assigned text is implied but not specifically stated. Students may often assume that as long as they acquire the necessary material that reading the text is merely an optional experience. By stating that course-related points are given for reading the textbook as assigned and in a timely manner, any misunderstandings are eliminated.   At the end of the semester, students sign a document on which they indicate the number of points (e.g., 80/100) that they are entitled to receive. Interestingly, students often downgrade the points they receive, as a matter of integrity, based upon the level of work that they have done, even at the cost of earning a lower grade.

Consider Using Journal Article Collections as an Alternative to Published Textbooks

With the advent of electronic databases, it is possible to create a customized, internet based reading collection of full-text articles from a variety of journals and authors. This practice provides a means for the selection of reading assignments that are more current and timely than textbooks, presents varied and opposing viewpoints on the topics of discussion, exposes students to the direct work of experts in the field, and provides a means for more in-depth investigations of key course issues. Generally speaking, a single textbook, which often has a short shelf life, cannot accomplish these outcomes.

Assure that Lectures Are only Supplements to Assigned Reading

Quite often, there is a high degree of overlap between the materials contained in assigned readings and the content of classroom lectures. Students are quick to realize this condition and draw the conclusion that listening in class (and perhaps taking notes) is a more efficient strategy than listening in class *and* reading the assigned materials. For faculty members, it is a good idea to conduct periodic checks to determine the level of overlap between lectures and readings.

Reference Lectures to Information and Illustrations Contained in the Course Texts

During classroom discussions and lectures, consider making frequent references to the materials covered in assigned textbooks. This strategy provides a coherent and comprehensive picture of course content and subtly reinforces the faculty member's commitment to both sources of learning and information.

Consider the Use of Occasional Open-Book Tests

There are times in every class and every discipline when the application of course content becomes more critical than recognition or recall of facts and concepts. At these times, students can be given questions or scenarios linked to the information contained in their textbook. The open textbook test reinforces the concept that the material contained in the textbook is important, and that it should be considered in the larger context of real world problem solving, application, and decision-making.

Give Quizzes on Assigned Reading Materials

One way of encouraging students to read the assigned course materials (e.g., text chapter, journal article, web-based information) is to schedule and implement specific accountability procedures. These accountability procedures can include group discussions and quizzes on the assigned reading or the requirement that students provide a brief written synopsis of the article or chapter's content and main points.

Provide Written Study Guides that Correspond with Assigned Course Readings

In every course, there are key pieces of information, concepts, and facts that are crucial (and that often form the core of examinations and evaluation procedures). Study guides provide students with a means for focusing their attention and effort. If a portion of the information contained in the study guide can only be found in the textbook, then students will need to explore and understand that information by using their textbook as a resource.

Raise Your Hand if You Are Here:
The Attendance Dilemma

At first glance, the question of whether attendance should be taken in college classrooms would seem to be a "no-brainer." It would seem to make perfect sense that a person spending (or borrowing) tens of thousands of dollars per year for the privilege of

attending college classes and earning a degree would logically choose to attend class on a regular basis. It would probably also be logical to assume that class attendance would dramatically contribute to enhanced levels of learning. Finally, going out on a limb, could we also assume that students, faculty members, and administrators would all agree that these propositions are reasonable and rational? Nothing could be further from the truth.

The flurry of discussion and activity around the issue of classroom attendance polices can be addressed from three different perspectives: 1) Political, economic, and cultural arguments, 2) The empirical evidence regarding the value of classroom attendance, and 3) Strategies for increasing student attendance patterns.

Political, Economic, and Cultural Arguments

Ironically, or so it would seem, many faculty members and students argue against the logic and necessity of attendance policies. Petress (1996) summarized some of the key arguments posed by these consumer groups:

- Students also assert themselves as customers and call on university officials to assure the college courses are solid enough to attract them to attend on a regular basis (i.e., make classes worth attending)
- Faculty resist the role of making distinctions between "excused" and "unexcused" absences

- Faculty frequently express concern about the procedural burden imposed by implementing a classroom attendance policy
- Faculty also raise the issue that mandatory attendance policies infringe on their academic freedom

Attendance policies are more than just a philosophical concern. They also play out rather dramatically in the worlds of culture and politics. Some universities, for example, have made a decision not to schedule classes on Fridays because those classes typically demonstrate poor attendance patterns. For students, this is a wonderful gift as it results in an abundance of "three day weekends." According to Young (2003), several universities are now in the process of "reclaiming Friday" as an instructional day of the college week.

In the political arena, the former New York City mayor Rudy Guiliani threatened to take $110 million dollars in city money away from the City University of New York because they failed to enforce classroom attendance policies.   In a sarcastic attack on school officials, Guiliani remarked, "You get a book like this. You put down the names of the students at the beginning of the semester. Then you call out their names at the beginning of class. And if they're there, you mark 'yes,' and if they're not, you mark 'no'" (Archibold, 1998, B4). It is safe to assume that as college costs rise and budgetary restrictions increase, there is an increasing probability of continued rhetoric on the issues of classroom attendance policies and their implementation. In reality, blogs, chatroom logs, and electronic polling devices are three of the many new ways to track attendance and participation while also responding to the lifestyles and learning preferences of millennial students.

As a final note concerning attendance and political, economic, and cultural arguments, it is relevant to note that today's students are tomorrow's employees. Good attendance is a critically important financial and productivity issue for employers (Paton, 2004).

Empirical Evidence Regarding the Value of Attendance Policies

Numerous research studies have investigated the relationship between the attendance patterns of college students and their levels of academic achievement and learning (Clump, Bauer, & Whiteleather, 2003). These studies have demonstrated that students who attend classes are often those who "regulate their own learning" (Van Blerkom, 2001). These are the intrinsically motivated students who feel an obligation not only to attend class but also to complete assigned readings, to pursue excellence in assignments, and to maximize the knowledge and skills that can accrue from a college education.

An interesting study by Moore (2003) reveals that students actually believe that better class attendance is a contributing factor in receiving a higher grade (and hopefully more learning). Moore's study also reveals that students think they should receive credit for attending class and that their final grade should be based upon what they know rather than whether or not they attend class. Overall, however, they also stated the belief that attending class in college is generally less important than attending classes in high school.

Strategies for Increasing the Level of Student Attendance

With the pressure to increase the levels at which students attend college classes, there has also been an effort to develop strategies for encouraging students to attend class. For millennial students, the question becomes whether the "carrot" or the "stick" is a better tool for facilitating regular class attendance patterns. Some of the ideas used in this regard include:

- Spend time at the beginning of the semester discussing the value and rationale for the course attendance policy (Moore, 2003)
- Give in-class quizzes on a regular basis (Thomas, 2002)
- Make classes more engaging and interesting for the students (Gump, 2005)

Specific methods for increasing attendance patterns in students, at this point, are largely anecdotal and generally lacking in empirical support. Here are some ideas for you to consider and evaluate in your own setting.

Include Your Course Attendance Policies in your Syllabi
It is important to advise your students of the policies that will govern attendance in your classes. They need to know your attendance expectations for the semester. Be clear and precise.

Clearly Articulate Your Attendance Expectations and the Related Consequences
If you choose to connect classroom attendance with certain consequences (e.g., grade or point total deductions), the parameters of those deductions need to be clearly and specifically defined. For example, students need to be aware of the specific number of "unexcused" absences that will result in lowering of their final grade and at what rate those deductions will occur. Develop a sound rationale for the penalties that will be enacted and confirm that these rules are consistent with university policies. If you believe that classroom attendance is important, talk with your students about your convictions and the reasons that lead you to require attendance as part of your expectations for classroom performance.

Consistently Collect and Record Attendance Data
To fairly administer a classroom attendance policy, it is of utmost importance that faculty members develop and implement reliable data collection strategies. Taking the time to correctly document and record attendance is a vital part of this process. It is strongly recommended that faculty document specific dates that students are absent from class. This

data will become invaluable in the event that a student appeals any actions that you have taken to penalize them for their absences.

Identify and Define Possible Exceptions to the Rules

It is a certainty that for every acceptable reason for an "excused" absence that you may define, students will invent and submit additional and previously undiscovered reasons why their requests are valid and reasonable. Sometimes the reasons are valid, other times they are not. Strive to be consistent in making these decisions.

Inform Students of Their Attendance Status

An attendance policy is intended to increase the likelihood that students will actually be in class. Develop a strategy for keeping students informed of their absence patterns. With the availability of electronic systems such as *Blackboard* or *CNet*, this has become an easy component of the total process.

Expect Requests for a Last Minute Reprieve

As the semester draws to a close, protests and questions will increase in number. Be prepared to respond in a manner that respects the dignity of students as well as the significance of regular class attendance. Administer your attendance policy consistently, fairly, and without malice. Be fair, yet firm. Always remember that the purpose of these procedures is to increase opportunities for student learning.

Expectations for Classroom Behavior

What levels and types of behavioral expectations are appropriate in the college classroom? This is a challenging and sensitive question for faculty members. It is simultaneously important that we identify the types of behaviors that are acceptable, and those that may pose a threat to the learning process. To further contemplate these reflections, let's throw in the issue of personal preferences: what are the behaviors that are significant enough to identify and discuss with students as opposed to those behaviors that are more in the category of our own personal biases or "pet peeves?"

There are several key issues in identifying and responding to those student behaviors that are a disruption to the learning process and challenge the limits of classroom civility. Part of this process is for each of us to identify the behaviors that fall outside the general rubric of "civility." As a first step, take the time to complete the inaugural version of "The Classroom Civility Inventory." Review the list of classroom behaviors and place a checkmark next to those that you believe would be disruptive or distracting in a classroom setting. As a guiding principle, those behaviors identified should be: 1) Behaviors that you consider important to being a good citizen in the learning community of your classroom, and 2) Behaviors that you would consider including in your course syllabus.

As a way of prioritizing your chosen responses and considering them in a larger context than your classroom, return to the list of items that you have identified with checkmarks. This time, circle the checkmarks placed next to items that are inappropriate in the classroom and that would also be considered inappropriate behaviors in most workplaces. This is an essential connection if we take seriously our role of preparing today's students to be tomorrow's citizens, leaders, and community members.

In his keynote address at a national conference on "Students in Transition" (2006), Scott Evenbeck, Dean of the University College at Indiana University-Purdue University Indianapolis, made the following observation about one of the greatest ironies of higher education practice:

> Behavior is a function of the person and the environment. So our entering students come to campus and we expect them to figure out our rules and our assumptions and our way of doing things. On campus, our philosophy is that students are adults. Children one day and miraculously transformed into adults the next. Really quite amazing. . .but we have this happy fiction that they will be adults who make choices and live with consequences and then will grow up and live happily ever after. You have to go to class when you're in high school and you have to go to work when you graduate. But when you're in college you can do what you want to do because you are an adult and we are moving you to the path of adulthood by treating you this way.

What Do You Expect?
"The Classroom Civility Inventory"

Place a checkmark by those behaviors on the following list that you believe are inappropriate in your classroom and that you will enforce through your syllabi and classroom procedures:

_____ Eating/drinking in class

_____ Overtly sleeping in class (i.e., head down or propped up with eyes closed)

_____ Using a laptop computer in class for purposes other than taking notes or participating in classroom activities (e.g., electronic games, email, Facebook, Google)

_____ Reading a textbook or other material that is unrelated to course content or classroom activities

_____ Talking out inappropriately to the extent that it is disruptive to the learning process

_____ Arriving late to class

_____ Leaving behind trash (e.g., cups, containers, wrappers)

_____ Wearing a hat or hood in class

_____ Talking with a neighbor during class to the extent that the volume of their voices becomes noticeably disruptive

_____ Overt, ongoing demonstrations of affection toward another student

_____ Text messaging or other forms of cell phone usage

_____ Inappropriate or rude comments to classmates or faculty during class discussions

_____ Other (specify) _____

_____ Other (specify) _____

If we are serious about preparing our students for life after college, then we have a responsibility to define the parameters of acceptable behavior (e.g., coming to class, demonstrating appropriate classroom social skills, respect for self and others). Likewise, we need to enforce those expectations in a fair, consistent, and reasonable manner — but enforce them. This level of seriousness about "civility," although just "one more thing that we have to do," is a valuable and important contribution that we can make to the lives of our students.

We must begin thinking about the expectations that we place on our students, how we determine those expectations, the manner in which we communicate them, and the strategies used to enforce them in a fair, reasonable, and humane manner.

Strategies for Promoting Civility in the Classroom

As a means of promoting the importance of civility in your college classroom, consider the following easy but important steps:

- **Create a List of your "Civility Expectations" for the Classroom** Think about what you consider to be most important, why you chose the individual items on the list, and if you are willing to expend the effort necessary to enforce those identified expectations.

- **Confirm the Validity and Fairness of your List** Consult with colleagues who will give you honest feedback on the listed behaviors. Ask them to assess the degree to which your expectations are consistent with the culture of the campus and the classroom.

- **Communicate your Expectations** Talk with your students in a variety of ways and at a variety of times about your expectations. At a minimum, it is necessary to include the list of desired behaviors in your course syllabus and to talk with your students about the rationale for these particular behaviors and the role of civility in their current and future lives.

- **Consistently Enforce Your Expectations** Now that you have determined and communicated your expectations, the next important step is to assure that you enforce these expectations in a consistent manner. Students typically expect and respect fairness in the administration of classroom and school rules. If we set a standard for behavior, we should also be willing to do the hard work of enforcing those rules. Remember the adage: "Praise your students in public and correct them in private."

Some Final Thoughts

Many time-honored maxims promote the value of prevention and planning. As faculty members, these words of advice should prompt us to look forward to the coming semester and make all of the necessary preparations to face the challenges ahead with a plan and a direction. Although this approach for teaching takes self-discipline and personal accountability, it is strongly suggested that any efforts you make to plan for the events of a semester will pay tremendous benefits in student learning, in the appreciation of your students, and last but not least, in your own mental health and sense of accomplishment.

CHAPTER THREE

Showtime!

W e now arrive at the heartbeat of instruction, the connection between the teacher, the student, and the instructional content as they interact in the classroom. Our daily challenge is how to design, develop, and implement classroom-learning experiences that engage students, invite them to learn, and capture their interest and imagination. Those outcomes may seem overwhelming. Take heart — they are possible to achieve!

In this chapter we will walk our way through the process of developing and implementing exciting, engaging, and interactive learning experiences. This process includes a number of valuable components, including:

- Lesson Planning and Flow
- Breaking the Ice
- Creating Instructional Learning Groups
- Group Management
- Facilitating Group Responses

Lesson Planning and Flow

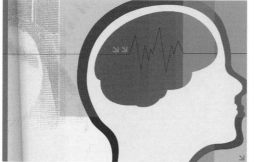

Think for a moment about an opportunity to spend 90 minutes per week over the course of the next three months with the most admired researcher and writer in your academic discipline. A series of seminars have been scheduled that will provide you with that opportunity. You and a group of twenty other faculty members will meet in a room with this renowned expert to learn about new developments and discoveries in your field. Are you excited? Of course you are!

The seminars begin with a 90-minute lecture. Questions begin to emerge in your mind. You also begin to think about the possibility of discussing, processing, and clarifying some of your newly acquired concepts and ideas. Those opportunities are not provided, so you sit dutifully and take copious notes on the lectures. The following week, at the next scheduled class period, this same pattern continues. In fact, throughout the entire seminar series, the format lends itself only to lectures and note taking. How might you feel at the end of this experience? At the seminar's conclusion, you may find yourself considering some of the following questions and observations in regarding the experience:

- I would have enjoyed the opportunity to share some of my own perspectives on the topics of discussion
- I wonder if the other participants in the seminar series found some of the explanations difficult to understand
- How does this information apply to my work
- I had some questions but felt uncomfortable asking them in front of the group

Over the course of the semester, you will undoubtedly spend time engaging in lectures with your students. That is part of the learning process. It helps, however, to have a specific template for thinking about the process of constructing a series of learning experiences for students that will transpire over the course of a semester. We will consider two approaches: 1) The Bookshelf Strategy, and 2) The Rule of Ten and Two.

The Bookshelf Strategy

The "Bookshelf" model provides students with an immediate opportunity "to practice what you are preaching" (Smith, Sheppard, Johnson, & Johnson, 2005). This approach assures that class presentations give students an opportunity to process their new learning and engage in critical thinking. As depicted in the graphic below, each class begins with an "Advance Organizer." Advance organizers are a collection of strategies that set the stage for instruction by advising learners of the topics, content, and focus of a class presentation. Based upon the early work of Ausabel (1963), a body of research has revealed that student learning increases dramatically when they are provided with a scaffold or framework that defines the nature of the learning experience. Advance organizers might include:

- A provocative question
- A famous quotation
- A story or news item
- A jointly developed "K-W-L" chart (i.e. What we know "K", What we want to learn "W", What we have learned "L.")
- A video clip, news article, picture, song, or quotation
- Any thought-provoking introduction that hooks the learner and encourages students to want to know more about the topic of discussion
- An acrostic. An acrostic is a poem or series of lines in which certain letters, usually the first in each line, form a name, motto, or message when read in sequence. Remember, for example, when you were in fourth grade and were asked to remember the names of the Great

Lakes (HOMES) or the colors in a rainbow (ROY G. BIV). These acrostics helped you retain this information. Provide your students with the opportunity to create their own acrostics as organizational and learning aids.

* Graphic organizers — A graphic organizer is a visual strategy (e.g., flow chart, visual/topical outline) for helping students remember important concepts and organize their thinking about varied interrelated concepts. To see the variety of graphic organizers that can be created, do a quick web search for "graphic organizers."

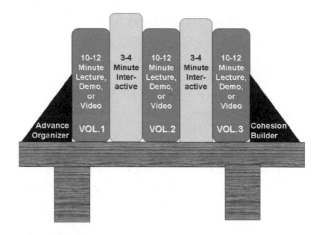

The selected advance organizer is followed by a series of interspersed segments of lecture (i.e., 10-12 minutes in length) and discussions/video clips/demonstrations (i.e., 3-4 minutes in length). When thinking about what to insert between the lecture segments, think about strategies that will encourage students to interact, discuss the content, clarify their understandings, and generate questions or concerns that may arise.

As we proceed through this chapter, you will see several examples of interactive strategies that can be applied in this portion of the instructional process. One very powerful strategy is "Paired Verbal Fluency" (Garmston & Wellman, 2002). This strategy starts with putting each student with a dialogue teammate. When the clock starts, Team Member #1 starts talking about the topic at hand and continues for 60 seconds. Then Team Member #2 talks for one minute, not repeating any of the information shared by their partner. Then it is Team Member #1's turn again; this time for 30 seconds of uninterrupted talking. And finally, Team Member #2 gets a final chance to talk for 30 seconds. This activity is surprisingly energizing and the students are usually amazed at how much they have learned and can remember.

The Rule of Ten and Two

Another consideration in the planning of a class lesson is the "Rule of Ten and Two" (Garmston & Wellman, 1999). This approach balances the time allocated for "teacher talk" and for "student processing." The Rule of Ten and Two states that for every ten minutes the teacher talks, students should be allocated two minutes to process the presented information and concepts.

Breaking the Ice

As each academic year begins it is always interesting to notice the behavior of college students as they take their seats on that much anticipated first day. There is often a general sense of stillness and uneasiness that fills the room. Students who otherwise might tend to be boisterous and laughing, take on a more serious and somewhat tentative demeanor. They watch as others enter the room, taking an occasional glance at the professor. During those awkward moments of waiting for class to begin, students wonder what the semester will hold, they ponder how much and how hard they will need to work, and maybe even give some thought to what they will learn. In spite of these initial feelings and behaviors, we also know that things do change as the semester proceeds. Students acclimate themselves to their surroundings, strike up friendships with

others in the class, and become more comfortable with the expectations, quirks, and behaviors of the professor.   Consider these strategies for "breaking the ice" on the first day of class.   The goals of these activities move beyond "party games" toward three important outcomes:

- Provide an environment in which students can form positive expectations about themselves as learners
- Create an energy and attraction to learning and to the subject matter that will be covered during the semester
- Begin the process of creating community

As you consider these strategies and the degree to which they may be applicable in your classroom, please consider the following guidelines:

- A key goal of the icebreaker is to build a level of comfort among your students; to create an environment where students feel accepted and valued and believe that they can be successful. This is a great way to start each new semester.
- Many millennial students are often reluctant to express their opinions in a classroom setting. There may be many explanations for this phenomenon.   It is logical to speculate that one reason is a fear that they will say something that would bring embarrassment.   The proposed icebreakers focus on getting students involved without forcing them to speak or share in any setting other than a small group.
- Having fun while learning together brings a positive outcome.   It is good to hear our students laughing and engaging with one another as they learn together as part of a community of scholars.
- Participating in icebreaker activities also provides you with a non-threatening means of getting to know your students. In addition, your students get to see you as a "real" person from the very beginning of the class.

The Name Game

Doesn't it feel great when you meet someone once and they remember your name? Our students feel the same way (Mittenforf, 2005). But how do we go about the process of remembering the names of students that we may only see once or twice a week? Here are some strategies:

- The old standby "Name Tent" that is placed on the table or desk each class
- Create a yearbook-style picture roster
- Ask students to create an index card sized "Passport" that includes their picture, likes and dislikes, their major, and something unique or interesting about themselves
- On the first day of class, tell the students that you are going to leave for five minutes. When you return, you expect each student to be able to introduce five other students on a first name basis and tell something interesting about the people they introduce. A class goal is to assure that all people are introduced at least once

People Search

Inviting students to participate in a "People Search" is a fun strategy for students to quickly interact with one another. This is, in a sense, a human scavenger hunt. Each member of the class is provided with a grid containing 12 squares (i.e., 3 columns and 4 rows). In each of the squares is a brief description of someone they need to search for in the room. Examples include:

- A person who is left handed
- Someone who has more than four siblings
- A person who is willing to stand on a chair and sing "Mary Had A Little Lamb"
- Someone who has lived in more than five states
- A person who was born outside the United States
- Someone who knows the names of the Seven Dwarfs
- A person who plays more than two musical instruments

- Additional ideas based upon your locale, the course, or the types of students that are part of the group

Students are given the task of circulating around the room looking for people who meet the criteria listed in the squares of their game sheet. When they find a person who meets one of the criteria, they ask that individual to sign their name in the appropriate square. The goal is to find signatures for each of the descriptors. An important ground rule is that each person in the room can only sign one other person's game sheet for a particular item.

Post-It Note Voting (Pebworth & Cooper, 1997)

You can probably remember students who sat through an entire semester in your class and never expressed an opinion or made a comment. It's not that they didn't have opinions, thoughts, or feelings, it's probably just a matter of not feeling comfortable in expressing those emotions and ideas in front of a group of their classmates. One way of involving all of your students is "Post-It Note Voting." Here are the steps:

- Create an imaginary continuum on the blackboard/whiteboard in front of the room with extremes like "Strongly Agree" and "Strongly Disagree"
- Give your students Post-It Notes of various colors
- Pose a question from your course or discipline that relates to current events in the world and requires a thoughtful or value-based response (e.g., "The minimum wage should be raised to $9.00 per hour;" "College tuition should be free for all individuals who wish to pursue a degree")
- Different colored post-it notes are used for each question.
- Students then post their responses along the continuum

Follow-up discussions about the trends and frequencies of various answers and the varied reasons people used for taking a strongly affirmative or negative position can be conducted in small groups.

"Permission" to Speak

There is often a natural separation that exists between faculty and students. One interesting way of connecting with students is to give them this direction: "I would like to get to know each of you, but quite often in a class this size it is difficult to initiate those connections. I encourage you to stop and introduce yourself when you see me on campus." You will be amazed at the number of students who take advantage of this "permission to speak" with you.

Creating Groups

The creation of learning groups is a key component of the interactive classroom. Students can work in groups that are transient in nature (i.e., a one-time matching or grouping for a specific activity or discussion) or more permanent in nature (i.e., groups that work together throughout the semester, grow deeper in relationships, and participate in the completion of long-term projects). Both types of groupings are valuable and should be routinely integrated into your teaching plan. Below you will find some creative strategies for creating student groups.

Round the Clock Learning Partners

Part of the genetic code of the human race seems to be a tendency to sit in the same seat every time we go into a classroom, meeting, or auditorium. In a classroom, this dynamic means that our students interact with the same individuals over the course of a semester. To promote opportunities for gaining different perspectives and for processing classroom content, students choose a series of "Round the Clock Learning Partners" (Garmston & Wellman, 2002).

At the beginning of the semester, students are presented with a line drawing of a clock indicating times between 1:00 and 12:00. They are asked to make appointments with twelve different classmates corresponding with each hour on the clock (i.e., a 1:00 partner, a 2:00 partner). As they arrive for class in subsequent weeks, they are asked to sit with a designated partner.

Seasonal Learning Partners

A variation of "Round the Clock Learning Partners" is the process of using "Seasonal Learning Partners" (Garmston & Wellman, 2002). In smaller classes, the same strategy applies with one minor modification. The students are given a paper with the four seasons of the year. They make appointments with four other people corresponding to the seasons of the year.

A "Sweet Way" to Create Groups

The "sweet way" begins as students arrive for class. They are asked to choose their favorite candy bar from a large bowl of miniatures (e.g., Snickers, Butterfinger, Milky Way). As class begins, students are then given the direction to create groups of four with the condition that each group must include members representing four different candy bar brands. Alternatively, you could suggest that students form a group of four with people who share their taste in candy bars (i.e., same choices). Let the groups begin!

Count Off

A common way of dividing a class into small groups is to ask the students to "count off" by fours, fives, sixes, etc. Since this technique often results in lackluster responses, try breathing new life into the process by:

- Asking students to count backwards (i.e., 5, 4, 3, 2, 1)
- Counting in a language other than English (e.g., uno, dos, tres . . .)
- Counting off by raising fingers to indicate their number (i.e., one finger, two fingers)
- Challenging the whole class to count off in a specified period of time (e.g., 20 seconds)

Group Management

I Have A Question

A tested teaching rule is that if a question is important enough to ask, then it merits the time necessary to wait for a response. Granted, the silence of waiting is sometimes uncomfortable. In time, however, students will learn that if you are going to ask a question, then you are also going to wait until someone provides a response.

Reflect and Respond

On occasion, there is a tendency to interpret silence as an indication that the students simply aren't thinking and don't want to answer. They may just need a few minutes to reflect on the question so that they can formulate an answer that they are willing to share with the rest of the group. For this reason, it is often wise to provide designated reflection time before asking anyone to go public with their response. So, for example, the teacher might say, "Take 60 seconds and think about this question. Write down a few thoughts that come to mind." Then, at the end of 60 seconds, the question can be posed for a large group response. Most often, the reflection time leads to several responses from the group.

Jigsaw

A jigsaw puzzle is a collection of many separate yet connected pieces of information. When assembled in the correct order and orientation, these pieces create a larger picture that is more complete than any of the component parts are able to depict on their own. This is a wonderful example of how cooperative learning capitalizes on the collective brain power of team 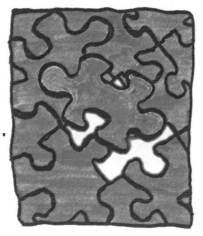 members with a resulting product that is better than any one of the team members could have imagined. In the "Jigsaw" strategy (Aronson, 1978), individual group members become experts in one aspect of the problem that the group is charged to address or resolve. Here is an example of how this might work in your classroom:

"How Can We Meet All of Their Needs? A Class-Wide Project"

Imagine that you are teaching a class that is considering the various options to resolve a pressing social problem: Reducing the prevalence of teen pregnancy. You assign members of the class to small groups of five. Advise the class that there are several different subgroups in the community that have expressed varied perspectives on the causes of teen pregnancy and the interventions that would be most appropriate to reduce their occurrences. These groups are: parents, school personnel, clergy, reproductive rights groups, and teens.

Five students work together as a group. They are designated as Team #1. Each of them are assigned (at the discretion of the group) to investigate the interests, concerns, and recommendations of one of the identified special interest groups (e.g., parents, teens). To do this, each of them will join with students from other subgroups (i.e., Team #2, #3, #4, #5) who are likewise investigating similar interests. So, for example, Student #1 is assigned to explore the concerns of parents. In that capacity, he meets with members of the other four class groups who also have an interest in the perspectives and opinions of parents.

After the subgroups connected with each of the specialty topics meet and discuss their area of interest, team members then return to their home group (i.e., Team #1, #2, #3, #4, #5) and share the information they have gained. The group then discusses the problem from these varied perspectives and constructs their own course of action through the process of consensus building. The jigsaw comes together as the pieces of information are shared, analyzed, and assembled.

From the "Jigsaw Classroom" website (http://www.jigsaw.org), we learn of the advantages that can accrue in regard to student learning:

What is the benefit of the jigsaw classroom? First and foremost, it is a remarkably efficient way to learn the material. But even more important, the jigsaw process encourages listening, engagement, and empathy by giving each member of the group an essential part to play in the academic activity. Group members must work together as a team to accomplish a common goal; each person depends on all the others. No one student can succeed completely unless everyone works well together as a team. This 'cooperation by design' facilitates interaction among all students in the class, leading them to value each other as contributors to their common task.

Graffiti

Graffiti is a strategy for encouraging groups of students to share their ideas in response to a problem or scenario and also to respond to the ideas of other student groups within the class (Abrami, 1995). This technique is easily implemented in the college classroom. As an example: A class is considering several different interpersonal challenges that may occur in the workplace and how they might respond. To facilitate discussion on this topic, divide the class into groups, each with five students. The faculty member has posted sheets of newsprint around the classroom, creating four separate learning stations (i.e., one on each wall). At each of these stations, an interpersonal relationship scenario has also been posted for student review, consideration, and response. Each group of students is provided with a marker of a different color. Group #1 begins at Station #1. Members of the group review the scenario at their station and provide a written response/solution on the newsprint paper. After a 5-10 minute period, the groups are directed to rotate in a clockwise fashion. Group #1 rotates to Station #2, etc. They read the presented scenario, read the previously posted responses, and provide additional suggestions or a modification of previously posted comments.

After each group has been given the opportunity to review and respond to each scenario, they return to their home station to reflect on the suggested responses to their presented dilemma. They then process these suggestions and formulate a composite response which they share with the entire group.

The "Graffiti" process allows members of the class to create original responses and consider suggestions that may enhance their own ideas surrounding the proposed question.

Minute Fingers

When students participate in group activities, it is often difficult for faculty members to accurately estimate the amount of classroom time that is appropriate for completing assigned tasks (Garmston & Wellman, 2002). Some groups finish before others, and in other situations we simply miscalculate the amount of time that it will take for a group to organize themselves and work together toward a common goal.

When the allotted time expires, and you notice that some of the groups have finished while others are still working, use the "minute fingers" technique. Ask each group to discuss how many additional minutes they will need (between 1 and 5) and then designate one person as their spokesperson. That person will raise a hand with the corresponding number of fingers extended to designate additional minutes needed. Survey the group and announce an average that meets the additional time needs of the groups in the class.

The Fickle Finger of Fate

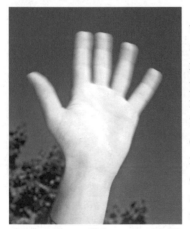

When students work in groups, there is often a need to designate specific individuals to fulfill varied roles. One way to facilitate this process is to bring the "fickle finger of fate" into play (Garmston & Wellman, 2002). After students are in groups, class members are asked to raise their right hand with the index finger extended. On the count of three, they are directed to point to the person in their group whom they feel would be the best possible recorder for the group's discussion. That person inherits the role of recorder. As a way of adding a positive spin to being designated as the recorder, that individual is given the privilege of choosing the person in their group who will serve as their spokesperson.

Facilitating Group Responses

An interesting dynamic occurs when working with students in groups. While small groups are working together, a buzzing sound will often fill the room as students interact and share ideas. Strangely and rather consistently, when you call the whole class back together to process their discussions, silence often fills the room when you ask "What kinds of ideas did you develop?" The following strategies assist in facilitating the transition between small group discussions and large group sharing.

Rotating Small Groups
Students rotate in small groups through a number of dialogue stations that have been created in the room. At each station, the small group ponders a question or issue, records its response on newsprint paper, and then moves to the next station. These groups will have an opportunity to respond to what the earlier groups thought and wrote (Brookfield & Preskill, 1999).

Snowballing
Students reflect on a question or issue by themselves. Then they pair with another student to share their thoughts and ideas. Next, two pairs of partners come together and form a group of four for the purpose of sharing. Finally, two groups of four can come together and form a group of eight. This allows for dialogue with a larger audience and the melding of ideas and concepts generated in the smaller group formats (Brookfield & Preskill, 1999).

"Speaking Up" Without Using Words
There are two common phenomena that can be observed in most classrooms: 1) The students who volunteer a response to most questions or topics, and 2) The students who will never volunteer a response to any question or topic. To level the playing field while encouraging all students to express their opinions, consider the use of two nonverbal opinion polls:

- **Standing in Response:** "If you agree with this position, please stand now."

- **Thumbs Up/Thumbs Down**: "If you agree, give a thumbs up; if you enthusiastically agree, wiggle your thumbs up sign. If you disagree, give a thumbs down; if you enthusiastically disagree, wiggle your thumbs down sign."

  Ask students to observe those around them who have both similar and different patterns of response. At the conclusion of the polling process on a variety of topically related questions, ask students to sit and talk with someone who agreed with them (or someone who disagreed with them). In either case, they are sharpening their thinking skills and processing the issues that surround and guide the questions.

A Change of Venue

There are times when it is necessary to provide an added impetus for the beginning of a discussion or dialogue. When this occurs, the teacher has a wonderful opportunity to infuse some excitement into the lesson by giving the students an unexpected assignment. For example, in a recent class the students appeared to be tired, uninvolved, and disengaged. They were generally unwilling to participate in discussions and, when pressed, would give very short and shallow responses to the questions that were being posed by the teacher. It was one of those painful moments in teaching. The students were placed into groups and given the assignment of creating a television commercial that illustrated the topic of discussion. New life and a renewed sense of energy filled the classroom.

In another class, things were dragging and the students were totally disengaged. Quite by surprise, they were asked to rearrange their chairs into rows similar to airplane seating (i.e., groups of two or three with an aisle down the middle). Students were assigned roles and randomly placed into the "airplane." The students were told that they had been randomly seated next to an individual for a two-hour airplane ride. Their assignment was to discuss the controversial topics of the day's lecture. Even though the topic and assignment had not changed, the change of seating and the simulated airplane scenario ignited a flurry of discussion and activity.

Give Me Five
There are times that we ask a question and get a quick and superficial response. One way to encourage students to dig deeper into the question is to challenge them to provide a specific number of additional responses to the question. At these times you would say, "That is a great answer! Let's think of five other reasons why . . ." (while holding up a hand with five fingers showing). As the students give their responses, manually count down to zero.

Designated Hitter
In this activity, students are placed into groups and given a list of discussion questions. As they discuss each question or topic, they are also asked to identify the individual in their group who will synthesize and share their team's responses with the larger group. This creates an immediate means for gaining summaries of the work and discussions of each small group.

Picture This . . . Or Sing It
As a way of capitalizing on the multiple intelligences in your classrooms, assign students to small groups and ask them to capture the major aspects of a concept or body of information in varied formats, such as a:

- Poster
- Rap, poem, or song
- Brief drama
- Television commercial
- News interview
- On-the-street interview
- Human sculpture
- Picture without words

You're a Poet and Don't Know It!

A great and often unexpected way of helping students process and summarize newly acquired knowledge is to encourage them to write poetry. One quick and easy type of poetry that students typically enjoy is the "cinquain." This is a five-line poem written in a number of formats. For example, one type of cinquain is written as follows:

- Line 1:   A title of one word or one subject
- Line 2:   Two words about the subject
- Line 3:   Three verbs that signify action
- Line 4:   Four words telling about your feelings for line one (words or phrase)
- Line 5:   A synonym for line one

An example may be helpful. Consider the topic of "pizza" and the poem that emerges from our thoughts about this important topic:

- Pizza
- Cheesy, Gooey
- Grab, Chomp, Savor
- Greasy pleasure and enjoyment
- Ecstasy

The writing of cinquain poetry can provide a great change-of-pace classroom activity. At the end of a lecture or section of course content, break the class into small groups and assign each group one key word or concept from which to develop a cinquain poem. Have the groups work together and then share the results of their creative thinking.

Group Response Cards

This strategy combines small group consensus building and the opportunity to gain a sense of the total group's response to issues of discussion. Each group of 3-5 students is provided with a series of response cards (e.g., Agree, Disagree, Not Sure). The faculty member then presents a scenario or problem situation for the class to consider and discuss in their small groups. At the signal, groups are asked to display their response cards. In this way, the faculty member can survey the responses and ask the groups to state their reasons for their chosen response.

This approach, of course, can be upgraded into a more technological framework by using one of the many "personal response systems" that are now on the market. This software provides students with the opportunity to respond to informational and opinion questions which are then tabulated and displayed for discussion and review.

Some Final Thoughts

Put yourself in the position of your students. If you were sitting in your classes, studying and learning about your chosen discipline, what would you want and expect from the faculty member teaching the class? This question should not be confused with the temptation of creating classes only from the perspective of what is pleasing to students. Rather, from a pedagogical perspective, effective teachers always evaluate their own performance based upon how well their students are learning. They feel an obligation to adapt instruction and provide instructional experiences that tap into multiple intelligences and learning styles of their students. Therefore, the question "What would it be like to be a student in your class?" is not a popularity-based question, but rather an assessment of instructional integrity. Take a few minutes to reflect on these questions as a guide to possible areas to consider in the quest to be the best possible teacher in a college classroom:

- What are the implicit and explicit expectations that I have for excellence on the part of my students as learners and for myself as their teacher?

- Am I consistently using a variety of teaching strategies that engage my students and promote their involvement in the learning process?

- What are the criteria that I use to determine whether chosen instructional strategies are appropriate and effective?

- Are there ongoing, direct, and relevant connections made between my chosen instructional content and the students' frames of reference?

- Do students have an expectation that the knowledge, skills, and dispositions they are acquiring can and should be applied in settings and circumstances beyond my classroom and this course?

- Do students have access to a variety of means for demonstrating their learning (i.e., different strategies and the opportunity to choose)?

CHAPTER FOUR

The Reviews:
Measuring the Impact of
Teaching on Student Learning

Another semester begins. Students wait expectantly as their professors review the course syllabus and describe learning objectives, required activities and assignments, and the procedures that will be used to assess their learning. In a vast majority of these classrooms, one of the primary means of assessing student learning will be some form of testing under the guise of tests, quizzes and examinations. For many of the over 15 million students enrolled in degree-granting institutions during a typical academic year, it is very likely that written examinations were a significant determining factor in assessing the degree to which they "learned" the required course content (often interpreted as their final grade). Extrapolating from the work of Milton (1986), if each of these students enrolled in an average of eight courses per year, and each course involved an average of two tests, there will be over 240 million tests given during a typical academic year. Testing is alive and well in higher education.

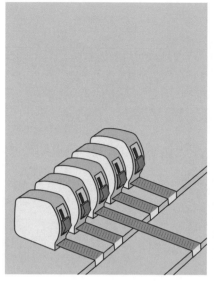

Given the rate at which tests are being used in college classrooms, one might be inclined to assume that this aspect of the educational process is both highly esteemed by faculty members and highly developed from a technical perspective. There is, however, a significant body of research and rhetoric indicating that college professors seemingly have a general sense of disdain for the rigors of test development and implementation (Burton & Miller 1999; Wergin, 1988). Although we are able to articulate what testing should be (e.g., reliable, valid, related directly to student learning), the gap between "what we say" and "what we do" is often very substantial (Angelo, 1999; Angelo & Cross, 1993; Berk, 1998; Brookhart, 1999a, Brookhart, 1999b; Ediger, 2002; Milton, 1986; Sanders, 2001).

Wergin (1988) candidly describes the state of affairs in classroom assessment as follows:

> If we have learned anything from educational research over the last fifty years, it is that students learn according to how they are tested. If we test students for factual recall, then they will memorize a set of facts. If we test them for their ability to analyze relationships, then they will begin to learn to think critically. If we assess how well they can apply classroom material to concrete problems, they will learn to do that. But despite the general agreement that classroom assessment procedures have a powerful influence over student learning, testing is the bane of most faculty members' lives. If college teaching is the only profession for which its members are never formally trained, then the way in which faculty evaluate students is perhaps the most glaring example of that deficit.

We all have personal horror stories of how inappropriate, even grotesque, college exams can be. (p. 5)

The evidence seems clear: There is an obvious need to rethink and revamp the procedures and techniques that are used to assess learning in the college classroom. This effort will require a willingness to analyze what has become standard practice and to think creatively in an effort to generate new ways to assess student learning.

Traditional vs. Alternative Assessments

Much of the discussion regarding classroom assessment has focused on the inherent differences between the somewhat loosely defined categories of "traditional" assessments and "alternative" assessments. Traditional assessment measures are typically written tests composed of objective questions in varying formats including true/false, multiple-choice, fill-in-the-blank, and matching (Montgomery, 2002). A key presumption of traditional assessments is the verifiability of a "correct" answer for each question. Although it is possible to construct traditional assessments that call on the learner to employ higher level thinking skills, most traditional assessments only require the student to recall (or perhaps even just recognize) and comprehend required information (Anderson, 1998; Cahn, 1994; Cameron, 1991; Montgomery, 2002; Sanders, 2001). Traditional assessments have been criticized from a variety of vantage points. First, critics often emphasize the fact that traditional assessments reinforce student learning in regard to isolated pieces of information. Second, traditional assessments provide limited opportunities for students to employ critical thinking skills in relation to course content. Third, it is arguably illogical to think that the information and concepts contained in 12 hours of lectures and 200 pages of reading can be reasonably condensed into 50 multiple choice questions. Finally, the fact that textbook publishers routinely offer ready-made "test banks" as a resource for faculty members simply reinforces the inclination to rely heavily on traditional assessment strategies with limited assurance that they are reliable or valid, or in fact contribute to student learning.   Given these caveats, can it be assumed that high test scores on traditional assessments are the best proof of student learning (Anderson, 1998; McDaniel, 1994; Murray, 1990; Sanders, 2001)? Supporters of the traditional mode of assessment generally focus their efforts on the process of creating the "good test" and emphasize the importance of reliability and validity in the mechanics of question construction.   As an example, a study by Haladyna, Downing, and Rodriguez (2002) focused on the validation of 31 "multiple choice item-writing guidelines" that they believe should be given serious consideration in the construction of classroom assessments. "Good test" proponents take very seriously the methodological aspects of assessment and the obligation of test developers to adhere to these conventions as opposed to the question of whether traditional assessments have a role in the university classroom.

Alternative assessments include a variety of techniques and strategies.   Davies and Wavering (1999) capture the wide range of options included in this category of assessment:

> The simplest definition for alternative assessment is a form of assessment other than traditional assessments, such as multiple choice and other usual forms of classroom assessment.   Such a definition leaves the door open for a range of assessment techniques. Examples of alternative assessment formats are: performance, portfolio, cooperative learning groups, peer teaching, exit cards, exhibitions, demonstrations of understanding, simulations, and observations, among others.   An important facet of many alternative assessment methods is that they are authentic and focus on process as well as product.   To be authentic means that the assessment mirrors applications of the assessed ability in real-life nonacademic settings. (p. 39)

The promotion of alternative assessment strategies is often approached from two perspectives: 1) A frontal attack on the perceived inadequacies of traditional assessments with a corresponding promotion of alternative assessment strategies (Anderson, 1998), or 2) The attachment of alternative assessment strategies to commonly valued theories of teaching and learning including constructivism, Bloom's taxonomy, multiple intelligences, and brain-based learning (Bostock, 1998; Davies & Wavering, 1999; Diaz-Lefebvre, 2004; McDaniel, 1994; Montgomery, 2002; Sanders 2001). Although the logical basis of alternative assessments is apparent, there have been limited attempts to create widely accepted methodological parameters for their use.

A Standard of Judicious Use

The debates rage on. Advocates for alternative assessment continue their systematic attacks on traditional assessment. Advocates for traditional assessment continue their quest for the perfect test. The end is nowhere in sight. What each group seems reluctant to acknowledge is the possibility that there is an integral role in higher education for both traditional and alternative assessments, that is, a "standard of judicious use." Rather than spending energy in the defense of a position, educators would be well advised to generate and refine a decision-making model that would assist faculty in determining the assessment technique that is most appropriate for the content, skills, and applications being taught.

There have been several attempts to create criteria for "good" testing practice. Angelo and Cross (1993) have proposed that classroom assessments should be teacher-directed, mutually beneficial (i.e., students in learning, faculty in the assessment of teaching), formative, context-specific (i.e., responsive to the needs and characteristics of students, teachers, and disciplines), ongoing, and rooted in good teaching practice. Wergin (1988) asserts that good practice in assessment results in 1) Improved teaching and learning, 2) A focus on what is maximally relevant, and 3) A mechanism for informing students about what they know or can do.

McDaniel (1994) has proposed that in the classroom of the future professors will need the skills necessary to:

- Define goals of instruction as measurable outcomes
- Concentrate on the kinds of outcomes — critical thinking, problem solving, creativity — that will serve the future citizen in a changing world
- Construct student evaluation opportunities that call for an integrating response
- Adjust time so that mastery is the goal
- Work to assure student success by using criterion-based rather than norm-based evaluation
- Redesign curriculum around priority outcomes to be demonstrated by students in a performance context (p. 30)

An analysis of these observations reveals a clear outcome-oriented emphasis on student learning and mastery. Additionally, it is relevant to note an emphasis on choosing assessment strategies that accomplish that goal rather than simply focusing on the means of assessment (i.e., traditional vs. alternative assessment). The time has come to move forward and create new options for assessment; options that are intentionally focused and designed to promote student learning.

A Variety of Assessment Strategies

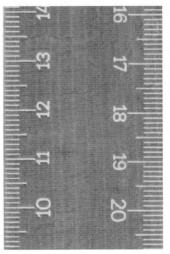

Consider the possibility of spicing up the approach that you take in assessment of classoom learning by trying one or more of the following alternatives.

Mix and Match

Students in Dr. Moore's "Sociology 101" class have an examination scheduled this afternoon. When the students arrive, they will be given 30 minutes to individually complete 50 questions (i.e., multiple choice and fill-in-the-blank formats). At the end of this 30-minute period, the students will be given an additional 10 minutes to interact with one another. During this part of the assessment process, the students can discuss and share their answers to the presented questions through one-on-one conversations. Changing an answer during this interactive period is completely acceptable. At the end of the class period, Dr. Moore will review the correct answers to each of the questions and engage students in dialogue about the rationale for their alternative responses.

Learning Partners

When students arrive in Dr. Ramirez's "Introduction to Economics" class tomorrow, they will participate in an examination covering Chapters 1-3 of the assigned text. As the students arrive, they will be randomly assigned a partner. During the 45-minute class period, the students will work cooperatively with their partners on completion of 60 multiple-choice questions. Each student will complete their own answer sheet but will also be free to discuss their opinions on the correct answers with their partner. After the examination is complete, students will retain their answer sheets as Dr. Ramirez reviews and discusses the correct responses (Parkyn, 1999; Pray & Tracy, 1999; Russo & Warren, 1999; Stearns, 1996).

Problem Solvers

Students in Dr. Watson's "Introduction to Nursing Practice" class are given a take-home examination that requires the development of written responses to various scenarios. To complete this exercise, students are assigned to a small group for the purpose of discussing the scenarios and developing the required written response. Each team will grapple with the presented problem and jointly develop a response. After each group completes the development of their written response, interactive strategies will be employed to assist the students in processing their written products. Teams are then reconvened and given the option of refining and expanding their original work. Teams will hand in their original and revised responses for review by the professor.

50/50

Students in Dr. Levinsky's "Introduction to Multicultural Education" participate in multiple assessment activities. At the conclusion of a unit of study, the students complete an on-line examination that includes  objective questions on the current topic of discussion. The software program used by Dr. Levinsky provides an opportunity for students to retake this portion of the examination as often as they choose. Only their highest attained score will be used in determining their course grade. The second component of the assessment process is completed in the classroom in small groups of two or three students. For this part of the assessment process, students are permitted to use their textbooks and class notes to cooperatively complete a series of questions that require application, evaluation, and synthesis of course content. Each portion of the assessment (i.e., objective on-line assessment, classroom-based cooperative learning activity) counts as 50% of the students' assigned grades.

"What's the Right Answer?"

There is a tendency to administer a classroom test and then simply provide students with their individual results in the form of a percentage, a letter grade, or the number of correct responses. This practice conveys a message that the score or result is of higher importance than the learning that may have occurred. If learning continues *during* the process of classroom assessment, students should be provided with an opportunity to compare their errant responses with those that are considered to be correct. On many occasions, these situations lead to rather unfortunate outcomes as described by Kher, Juneau, and Molstad (2002):

> Most faculty have had the experience of returning graded tests
> and leading a protracted discussion of test items and alternative

interpretations of each, and the rationale for the "correct" answers. When class ends the teacher is as relieved as a soldier returning from battle. Students who previously showed positive regard for the faculty member often become confrontational when arguing to upgrade their test scores. (p. 148)

In spite of these realistic cautions, even the bravest of faculty face the sharing of "correct" answers with fear and trepidation. Consider, however, the following scenarios and their implications for student learning.

Scenario #1. Tomas, a science major, has just completed taking a mid-term examination in the course "Introduction to Chemistry." The test was comprised of multiple choice, fill in the blank, and true/false questions. As he left the class one of his best friends asked Tomas, "How did you do on the test?" Tomas responded, "I'm not sure, but I think that I did OK." One week later, Dr. Smith posts the grades for the examination revealing only the percentage of correct responses attained by each student. Tomas learns that he was able to provide correct responses on 86% of the questions. Unfortunately, he will never be sure of the correct answers to the 14% of the items that he missed, or for that matter, which 14% of the items he missed and which he answered correctly.

Scenario #2. Courtney is enrolled in the course "History of World Civilizations." Her professor, Dr. Winchester, recently administered an examination that was comprised of 100 multiple choice items. Much like Tomas, when Heather left the classroom she had mixed feelings about her performance on the test. Unlike Dr. Smith, it is a common practice for Dr. Winchester to devote class time immediately after every examination to review the questions and appropriate answers. On occasion, this process results in vigorous debates and disagreements between the students and Dr. Winchester. She does not take this personally and looks forward to the interchange of ideas and the opportunity to observe her students wrestling with the key concepts and big ideas in history. On occasion, Dr. Winchester has determined that some of the answers advocated by her students are appropriate responses to the test items and could be considered correct. She gives students credit for those answers and celebrates the learning that has taken place in her classroom. Further, her students have a better understanding of the course content.

According to Aldrich (2001) the process of returning examinations can be made less painful by following a logical progression of rules: 1) Provide the students with the grading key, 2) Hand back the examinations at the beginning of the next class as a means of demonstrating their importance, 3) Ask the students to meet in small groups to discuss and review the questions and answers, 4) Provide the students with an opportunity to take a short quiz that is comprised of questions from the most recent examination, and 5) Make the final examination a cumulative experience as a means of increasing motivation to obtain and understand the "correct answers." The results of this process are described as follows:

> When I first began teaching, more than thirty years ago, the experience I dreaded more than any other was handing back graded exams . . . . Today, I look back at those early years and wonder, 'What was I thinking?' I have changed my approach to the day after exams. Instead of feeling anxiety about my performance, I now focus on the student's performance and the use of the next class to push the learning process forward. (p. 82)

In order to make the written assessment process a valid learning experience, it is important that students be provided with opportunites to learn and discuss the answers to presented evaluation tasks. This opportunity could even be taken to a higher level by allowing students to retake the examination and reinforce the concepts and information that they have acquired (Hamilton, 2003; Murray, 1990; Toma & Heady, 1996).

Second Chances

The "Second Chance" strategy involves giving students an opportunity to retake the same (or if you wish, a similar) examination. This privilege can be a freebie, or can be tied to some other course requirement such as perfect attendance. Students who take advantage of this opportunity are given a grade that is the average of their performance on the two test administrations.

The Question Bank

To promote the most critical aspects of course content, students are provided with a bank of potential test questions for which they must find the answer. Quite often, text publishers will provide a bank of test questions that accompany course texts. Students can then read along in the text and find the answers to the presented questions. Actual test items are selected from this bank of questions.

The Essay Bank

Students are provided with a list of potential essay questions. The actual test is comprised of a number of items from the presented sample essays.

The No Fault Quiz

As reported by Sporer (2001), students often ask the question, "Can I get extra credit?" One way to provide this opportunity in a meaningful way is the "No Fault Quiz." Students are given a 5-15 question quiz (i.e., multiple choice, true/false, fill-in-the-blank) covering the previous week's content. Points gained on the No Fault Quiz count as extra credit, and points that may be "missed" do not count against the student. Answers to the questions are provided immediately after the quiz. Student performance is recorded, but students take away the quiz questions that can later serve as a source for review.

Take Your Pick

Typically, course syllabi specify the assignments that students are expected to complete during the semester and the date that each assignment is due. An alternative is the "Take Your Pick" strategy. At the beginning of the semester, students are provided with a list of the assigned projects, papers, and presentations that are to be completed. Instead of providing specific due dates for each assignment, the instructor provides a series of "Hand-In Dates" (e.g., Completion Date #1,

Completion Date #2). Students choose the order in which they complete the assigned tasks for the semester and are merely required to submit one completed assignment on each of the designated "Completion Dates." This provides students with an opportunity to make decisions about which assignments they can complete first and which assignments will require the greatest amount of time to complete. Additionally, this strategy provides an opportunity to "front load" assignments and prevents the common practice of requiring a massive amount of completed work during the final two weeks of the semester.

Exit Cards

In a recent article, Davies and Wavering (1999) describe a procedure for encouraging students to engage in ongoing reflection about their learning. "Exit Cards" provide a strategy for students to process what they are learning and to apply that information to their chosen discipline of study. On a weekly basis, students are asked to complete a 5 x 8 card which contains two questions: "So What?" (designed to elicit a summary of the main points that were discussed and reviewed during the week) and "Now What?" (that requires students to relate that content to their lives, learning, and future roles).

Some Final Thoughts

As you think about the ways in which you assess the learning of your students, consider moving beyond the bounds of multiple choice tests and information that can be reduced to the realm of a scantron sheet. There is much more to learn and assess. Provide your students with the opportunity to take the wealth of information that you are providing, wrestle with it, be creative with it, and use it in novel ways. Those activities, although somewhat unconventional in the realm of classroom assessment, will energize your students in ways that you never imagined and will provide you with a multitude of ways to assess their learning.

References

Abrami, P. C. (1995). *Classroom connections: Understanding and using cooperative learning.* Toronto: Harcourt Brace.

Aldrich, H. E. (2001). How to hand back exams to your class. *College Teaching, 49,* 82.

Anderson, R. S. (1998). Why talk about different ways to grade? The shift from traditional to alternative assessment. *New directions in teaching and learning, No. 74.* San Francisco: Jossey-Bass.

Angelo, T. A. (1999, May). Doing assessment as if learning matters most. *AAHE Bulletin,* 1-5.

Angelo, T. A., & Cross, K. P. (1993). *Classroom assessment technique.* San Francisco: Jossey-Bass.

Archibold, R. C. (1998, April 25). Yes, teacher: Giuliani scolds CUNY on attendance policies. *New York Times,* p. B4.

Aronson, E. (1978). *The jigsaw classroom.* Beverly Hills, CA: Sage Publications

Ausabel, D. P. (1963). *The psychology of meaningful learning.* New York: Grune and Stratton.

Barr, R. B., & Tagg, J. (1995). From teaching to learning — A new paradigm for undergraduate education. *Change, 27*(6), 12-25.

Berk, R. A. (1998). A humorous account of 10 multiple-choice test-item flaws to clue testwise students. *Journal on Excellence in College Teaching, 9,* 93-117.

Bosman, J. (2006, February 3). Two women's magazines shift focus to 'millennials'. *New York Times,* p. C3.

Bostock, S. J. (1998). Constructivism in mass higher education. *British Journal of Educational Technology, 29,* 225-240.

Brandenburg, M. M. (2005). Solutions exist for next-generation planners. *Journal of Financial Planning, 18*(9), 21.

Braskamp, L. A., Trautvetter, L. C., & Ward, K. (2006). *Putting students first: How colleges develop students purposefully.* Bolton, MA: Anker.

Brookfield, S. M., & Preskill, S. (1999). Strategies for reporting small-group discussions to the class. *College Teaching, 47,* 140.

Brookhart, S. M. (1999a). Classroom assessment: Tensions and intersections in theory and practice. *Teachers College Record, 106,* 429-458.

Brookhart, S. M. (1999b). *The art and science of classroom assessment: The missing part of pedagogy.* Washington D.C.: ERIC Clearinghouse on Higher Education.

Burton, R. F., & Miller, D. (1999). Statistical modeling of multiple-choice and true/false tests: ways of considering, and of reducing, the uncertainties attributable to guessing. *Assessment and Evaluation in Higher Education, 24*(4) 399-412.

Cahn, S. M. (1994). Rethinking examinations and grades. In P. J. Markie (Ed.) *A professor's duties: Ethical issues in college teaching,* (pp. 171-192). Lanham MD: Rowman and Littlefield.

Cameron, B. J. (1991). Using tests to teach. *College Teaching, 39*(4), 154-156.

Clump, M. A., Bauer H., & Bradley, C. (2004). The extent to which psychology students read textbooks: A multiple class analysis of reading across the psychology curriculum. *Journal of Instructional Psychology, 31,* 227-232.

Clump, M. A., Bauer, H., and Whiteleather, A. (2003). To attend or not to attend: Is that a good question? *Journal of Instructional Psychology, 30,* 220-224.

Connor-Greene, P. A. (2000). Assessing and promoting student learning: Blurring the line between teaching and testing. *Teaching of Psychology, 27,* 84-88.

Davies, M. A., & Wavering, M. (1999). Alternative assessment: New directions in teaching and learning. *Contemporary Education, 71,* 39-46.

Diaz-Lefebvre, R. (2004). Multiple intelligences, learning for understanding, and creative assessment: Some pieces to the puzzle of learning. *Teachers College Record, 106,* 49-57.

Downing, K. (2006). Next generation: What leaders need to know about the millennials. *Leadership in Action, 26*(3), 3-6.

Ediger, M. (2002). Problems in grading based on testing university students. *College Teaching, 36,* 37-40.

Evenbeck, S. (2006, November). Centering on students. Paper presented at the 13th Annual Conference on Students in Transition, St. Louis, MO.

Garmston, R. J., & Wellman, B. M. (1999). *The adaptive school: A sourcebook for developing collaborative groups.* Norwood, MA: Christopher-Gordon Publishers.

Garmston, R. J., & Wellman, B. M. (2002). *The adaptive school: Developing collaborative groups.* Norwood, MA: Christopher-Gordon Publishers.

Garner, J. B. (2007, April). *Lecture induced mind paralysis.* Presented at the International Conference on Teaching and Learning, Jacksonville, FL.

Garner, J. B., & Pattengale, J. (2007, February). *The Wiki world of millennial students.* Presented at the meeting of the National Resource Center for the First Year Experience, Dallas, TX.

Gump, S. (2005). The cost of cutting class: Attendance as a predictor of student success. *College Teaching, 53,* 21-26.

Haladyna, T. M., Downing, S. M., & Rodriguez, M. C. (2002). A review of multiple-choice item-writing guidelines for classroom assessment. *Applied Measurement in Education, 15,* 309-334.

Hamilton, T. M. (2003) (or 1999). Everyone deserves a second chance: Using the day after the exam as a learning opportunity. *College Teaching, 51,* 21.

Howe, N., & Strauss, W. (2000). *Millennials rising: The next great generation.* New York: Random House.

Howe, N., & Strauss, W. (2006). *Millennials and Pop culture.* Great Falls VA: LifeCourse Associates.

Howe, N., & Strauss, W. (2003). *Millennials go to college.* Washington DC: American Association of Collegiate Registrars.

Hutchings, P., & Shulman, L. S. (1999). The scholarship of teaching: New elaborations, new developments. *Change, 31*(5, 11-15).

Jayson, S. (2006, September 28). Round and round they go. *USA Today,* p. 8.

Johnson, D. W., & Johnson, R. T. (1993). *Cooperation in the classroom.* Alexandria, VA: Association for Supervision and Curriculum Development.

Kher, N., Juneau, G., & Molstad, S. (2002). Test feedback class sessions: Creating a positive learning experience. *College Teaching, 50,* 148-150.

Littlefield V. M. (1999). *My syllabus? It's fine. Why do you ask? Or the syllabus: A tool for improving teaching and learning.* Paper presented at the Society for the Improvement of Teaching and Learning, Calgary, Alberta, Canada.

Marinelli, D., & Pausch, R. (2004, March 19). Edutainment for the college classroom. *Chronicle of Higher Education,* p. B16.

McDaniel, T. R. (1994). College classrooms of the future. *College Teaching, 94,* 27-32.

Millard, B. (2007). *Explorer's guide: Starting college with a sense of purpose.* Dubuque: Kendall Hunt Publishing.

Milton, O. (1986). *Will that be on the final?* Springfield IL: Charles C. Thomas.

Mittendorf, J. (n.d.). Learning student names. Retrieved December 14, 2005 from http://www. ntlf.com/html.lib/bib/names.htm.

Montgomery, K. (2002). Authentic tasks and rubrics: Going beyond traditional assessments in college teaching. *College Teaching, 50*(1), 34-39.

Moore, R. (2003). Attendance and performance: How important is it for students to attend class? *Journal of College Science Teaching, 32,* 367-371.

Murray, J. P. (1990). Better testing for better learning. *College Teaching, 38,* 148-153.

Nelson, B. (2005). Here come the millennials. *Corporate Meetings and Incentives, 24*(3), 50.

Parkyn, D. L. (1999). Learning in the company of others. *College Teaching, 47,* 88-90.

Paton, N. (2004, July 13). From absence to attendance. *Personnel Today,* p. 25.

Pebworth, M., & Cooper, G. (1997). The poster/post-it activity. *College Teaching, 45,* 7-10.

Petress, K. (1996). The dilemma of university undergraduate student attendance policies: To require class attendance. *College Student Journal, 30*(3), 387-389.

Pray, S. M., & Tracy, D. M. (1999). Collaborative essay testing. *College Teaching, 47*(1), 33-36.

Prensky, M. (2001). Digital natives, digital immigrants. *On the Horizon, 9*(5), 1-2.

Reda, S. (2006). RU ready? *Stores Magazine, 88* (11), 10-20.

Romano, A. (2006). Young adults tune in. *Broadcasting and Cable, 136* (26), 19.

Russo, A., & Warren, S. H. (1999). Collaborative test taking. *College Teaching, 47,* 18-20.

Sanders, L. R. (2001). Improving assessment in university classrooms. *College Teaching, 49,* 62-64.

Scott, C. (2005, October 7). The net generation in the classroom. *Chronicle of Higher Education,* pp. A34-37.

Seckler, V. (2006, January 11). Catch the millennials if you can. *Women's Wear Daily,* p. 10.

Sikorski, J. F., Rich, K., Saville, B. K., Buskist, W., Drogan, O., & Davis, S. F. (2002). *Teaching of Psychology, 29,* 312-313.

Slattery, J. M., & Carlson, J. F. (2005). Preparing an effective syllabus. *College Teaching, 53,* 159-164.

Smith, K. A., Sheppard, S. D., Johnson, D. W., & Johnson, R. T. (2005). Pedagogies of engagement: Classroom-based practices. *Journal of Engineering Education, 94,* 87-101.

Spence, L. D. (2001). The case against teaching. *Change, 33* (6), 10 – 19.

Sporer, R. (2001). No-fault quiz. College Teaching, *49,* 61.

Stearns, S. A. (1996). Collaborative exams as learning tools. *College Teaching, 44,* 111-112.

Tagg, J. (2003). *The learning paradigm college.* Bolton, MA: Anker.

Thomas, B. (2002, June 21). If I quiz them . . . they will come. *Chronicle of Higher Education, 48* (41), p. B5.

Thompson, J. A., & Grabau, A. (2004). A la carte grading: Providing students opportunities to determine their own paths to success. *Journal of Natural Resources and Life Sciences Education, 33,* 92.

Toma, A. G., & Heady, R. B. (1996). Take-two testing. *College Teaching, 44,* 61.

Twenge, J. M. (2006). *Generation me.* New York: Free Press.

Van Blerkom, M. L. (2001). Class attendance in undergraduate courses. *The Journal of Psychology, 126*(5), 487-494.

Wergin, J. F. (1988). Basic issues and principles in classroom assessment. In J. H. McMillan (Ed.), *Assessing student's learning* (pp. 5-17). San Francisco: Jossey-Bass.

Young, J. R. (2003, April 18). Reclaiming Friday: Several colleges try to bring back academic life to the last weekday. *Chronicle of Higher Education, 49*(32), p. A46.

Notes

Notes

Notes

Notes